ALL THIS INSIDE...

LittleBrother

Published 2017. Little Brother Books Ltd, Ground Floor, 23 Southernhay East, Exeter, Devon, EX1 1QL
Printed in Poland
books@littlebrotherbooks.co.uk   www.littlebrotherbooks.co.uk
The Little Brother Books trademark, email, website addresses are the sole and exclusive properties of Little Brother Books Limited.

WELC

FOLLOW MY LEAD!

SWEET AS CANDY!

...to a world where babies run everything, little Rockers rebel against naptime and Teacher's Pets become class presidents with 'Free Pizza Fridays'!

DIAMONDS ARE MY BFF

© MGA

Inside this awesome Activity Annual the L.O.L. world has been brought to life with fierce activities, sassy quizzes and crafts that are totally on point. You'll find all your favourite Dolls and, of course, a surprise or two along the way!

SURPRISE NAME

What's your L.O.L. Surprise name? And which club do you belong to? Answer the three questions below and all will be revealed!

FIRST NAME

WHAT'S YOUR FAVOURITE COLOUR?

TICK A STAR TO ANSWER EACH QUESTION.

SECOND NAME

WHICH MONTH WERE YOU BORN?

Blue	☆	Spice
Pink	☆	Posh
Purple	☆	Cosmic
Green	☆	Royal
Gold	☆	Fresh
Turquoise	☆	Super
Black	☆	Fancy
Grey	☆	Glitter
Yellow	☆	Miss
Silver	☆	Honey
Red	☆	Cozy
White	☆	D.J.

January	☆	B.B.
February	☆	Champ
March	☆	Punk
April	☆	Queen
May	☆	Baby
June	☆	Q.T.
July	☆	Sk8er
August	☆	Captain
September	☆	Babe
October	☆	Swag
November	☆	Dancer
December	☆	Bae

MY L.O.L. NAME IS:

....

MY CLUB IS:

....

WORK IT, BB!

MAKEOVER!

CLUB

WHAT'S YOUR FAVOURITE ANIMAL?

Dog	☆	The Glitterati
Elephant	☆	Opposites Club
Tiger	☆	Spirit Club
Rabbit	☆	Storybook Club
Dolphin	☆	Glee Club
Monkey	☆	Athletic Club
Tortoise	☆	Dance Club
Panda	☆	Glam Club
Cat	☆	Theatre Club
Frog	☆	Cosplay Club
Flamingo	☆	Hip Hop Club
Owl	☆	Chill Out Club
Hamster	☆	Retro Club

MISS BABY

FIND YOUR BFFS

CLUB NAME

WHAT WE'RE ALL ABOUT

WHAT WE LIKE TO DO

HOW WE'RE UNIQUE AND FIERCE

OUR FAVOURITE THING TO SAY

THE MOST SURPRISING THING ABOUT OUR CLUB

Think of your favourite things to do then create an L.O.L. club that's totally you!

Now design an awesome new look for your club members:

© MGA

#DROP THE MIC

Who do you turn into when you've got a mic in your hand? Take this fun quiz to reveal your karaoke style!

Do you dream of superstardom? — N

Do you play your music LOUD? — N

Does performing rock your world? — N

Y

Y

Y

Do you ever get stage fright?

Do you bust a move when you hear a good tune?

Do song lyrics stick in your head?

Y

N

N

Y

N

Y

Do you like to stand out from the crowd?

Can you play an instrument?

Do you adore being in the spotlight?

Y

N

Y

N

Y

N

SOLO DIVA
You adore the limelight and don't wanna share your moment of fame. Singing your heart out with a big solo number is your karaoke dream.

ROCKSTAR
You love loud music and thumping beats. Your karaoke style is belting out a rock classic, preferably while strumming a guitar.

GIRL GROUP
You think karaoke should be fun and don't take yourself too seriously. Crooning along with your BFFs is your singing style.

SONG SURPRISE

Grab your mic and help the Hip Hop Club fit these song titles into the crossword. Then de-code the hidden surprise below!

EACH SONG TITLE WILL ONLY FIT IN ONE PLACE.

TIME TO PARTY

WORK IT

GLAM IT UP

HOW WE ROLL

WISH

SHAKE IT

CANDY

DANCE IT OUT

HIDDEN SURPRISE

REARRANGE THE LETTERS IN THE PINK SQUARES TO REVEAL THE NAME OF ONE OF THE HIP HOP CLUB. WRITE YOUR ANSWER BELOW.

#SELFIE SECRETS

Selfie game strong! Miss Baby has the lowdown on how to take the perfect selfie. Forget the rest, learn from the best!

WORK IT, GIRL!
Practise lots of selfie poses in front of the mirror so you know what works for you. But don't forget, when the time comes it's all about being natural!

PUT A SASH ON IT

I GOT UR BACK!
Think about what's behind you – either find an interesting setting for your pic or keep the background clear.

BLUR-FREE ZONE!
Hold your phone steady for a perfectly focussed shot.

SO EXTRA!
Use props to add interest to your pic – sunglasses, headwear and food are all failsafe accessories.

MISS BABY

©MGA

SHOCK FACTOR!
Add a surprise element to your pic that people won't be expecting, such as an unusual backdrop, a funny prop or crazy hair.

DON'T GO IT ALONE!
Solo selfies are so last year - grab some friends and go for a group selfie instead.

EASY DOES IT!
Don't take squillions of photos to get the perfect shot – some of the best selfies are one-off, spur of the moment pics.

GET UR GLOW ON!
Take your selfie in natural lighting for a flattering glow. Fluorescent lighting is nobody's friend!

LOOKING GOOD!
Always take your picture from above for a more flattering angle.

BEE YOUR SPARKLY SELF!
Don't take yourself too seriously. Smile, goof around if you want to – selfies should be fun!

©MGA

SCREEN SMASH

Oops, Queen Bee has dropped her phone. Put the broken pieces back together so she can see who's calling but beware, not all the pieces fit!

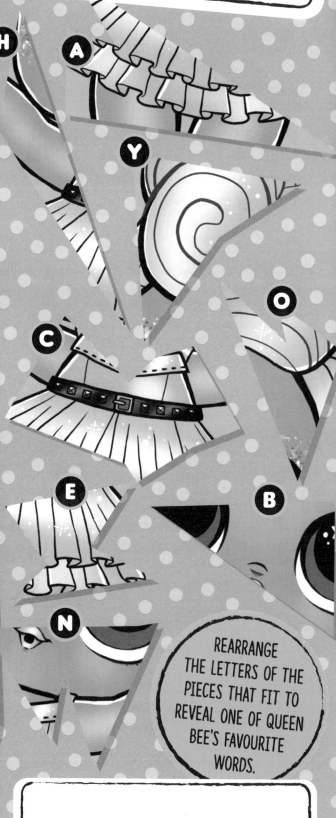

REARRANGE THE LETTERS OF THE PIECES THAT FIT TO REVEAL ONE OF QUEEN BEE'S FAVOURITE WORDS.

CHILLIN'

The Chill Out Club are so cool they're almost frozen! Can you help them spot these chilly words in the wordsearch below?

```
F S N O W M A N E   E
R S Y Z O C B K Y   R
E L B R R R A R L   L
E E C I R L R H L   I
Z D I T F S S C I   H
I G O W L O D I H   C
N E O N P H E R C   Y
G N E F R O S T Y   Y
S L L A B W O N S
```

ANSWERS ON PAGE 48.

SNOWFLAKE

ICE

SLEDGE

COZY

SNOWMAN

CHILLY

POSH

FREEZING

SNOWBALL

FROSTY

BRRR

SNOW ANGEL'S SURPRISE

Once you've found all the words in the wordsearch write the letters you haven't used below. Copy them in the order they appear in the wordsearch and they will reveal a secret message from Snow Angel.

....

....

©MGA

IT'S SHOWTIME!

KEY

A =    N =

B =   O =

C =   P =

D =   Q =

E =   R =

F =   S =

G =   T =

H =   U =

I =   V =

J =   W =

K =   X =

L =   Y =

M =   Z =

The Theater Club are keeping the storyline of their latest play under wraps but don't mind letting you in on the secret! Crack the code to reveal the plot.

CHECK MEOWT

The plot...

ANSWERS ON PAGE 48.

SAY THAT AGAIN!

The L.O.L. Dolls are always ready with a sassy saying! Draw a line to link the quotes to the right babies?

ANSWERS ON PAGE 48.

STRAIGHT A'S 4 EVA!

WHAT'S THE BUZZ HONEY?

QUEEN BEE

ROCKER

CHILLIN' WITH MY HOMIES!

KITTY QUEEN

QUEEN OF THE RINK.

TEACHER'S PET

I ROCKED B4 I COULD WALK!

BRRR B.B.

PURR-FECTION!

ICE SK8ER

©MGA

SCRAMBLED SURPRISE!

ANSWERS ON PAGE 48.

Oops, the babies' names have been mixed up. How quickly can you unscramble them? #Ticktock

DAIV ➊ ....

USRFER ABBE ➋ ....

CNETER SGATE ➌ ....

NEYHON NUB ➍ ....

IKKCS ➎ ....

CYHRRE ➏ ....

5 minutes +
You might wanna practise your unscrambling skills!

2 to 4 minutes
You're hot on the heels of Teacher's Pet!

Less than 2 minutes
A* for you, awesome unscrambler!

©MGA

EXPLODING SURPRISE!

YOU WILL NEED

FOUR SHEETS OF DIFFERENT COLOURED PAPER

A RULER

A PENCIL

SCISSORS

GLUE

STICKERS TO DECORATE

A SMALL GIFT

How do you unbox? This super-cool explosion gift box is THE most surprising way to unbox a present! Here's how to make your own…

YOUR MESSAGE!

1
LET'S START!
Draw a square 21cm x 21cm on a piece of coloured paper. Divide each side into three marking each 7cm segment with a dot. Use the ruler and pencil to draw lines to join the dots so that your square is divided into nine smaller squares.

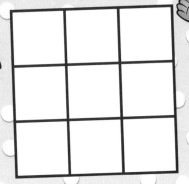

2
Cut out and discard the four corner squares so that you're left with a cross shape. Fold the outside squares in following the dotted lines lines shown here.

©MGA

BOX LID

Fold the blue **lines**
Cut the orange **lines**

WARNING!

ALWAYS GET HELP FROM A GROWN UP WHEN USING SHARP SCISSORS.

GLUE HERE

GLUE HERE

GLUE HERE

GLUE HERE

MESSAGE LAYER

GLUE THIS SIDE DOWN AND WRITE YOUR MESSAGE ON THE OPPOSITE SIDE!

Fold the blue **lines**
Cut the orange **lines**

BREAKIN' HEARTS AND TAKIN NAMES

3

DO IT AGAIN!
Repeat steps 1 and 2 with three more squares of coloured paper measuring 19.5cm x 19.5cm, 18cm x 18cm and 16.5cm x 16.5cm. You'll end up with three more cross shapes, each one slightly smaller than the one before.

4

TIME TO GET CREATIVE!
Decorate your four cross shapes with cut-out shapes, or stickers.

5

GETTING CLOSER!
Cut out the message layer on page 19 and fold along the blue dotted lines - this will give you a fifth cross. Write a message in the middle square.

6

Take your biggest cross shape and put some glue in the centre square. Stick the next biggest cross shape onto it. Repeat until all four cross shapes are glued on top of each other in size order. Finally glue on the fifth cross shape (your message layer) so that your message is visible on the top.

7

ALMOST THERE!
Almost there! Cut out the box lid on page 19 along the black lines. Cut along the orange lines and fold in the tabs along the blue lines. Glue the tabs together to make the corners of the lid.

8

EXCITED YET?
Fold the outsides of your cross shapes in to make a box shape and put the lid on top to hold it closed. Decorate the lid and the outside of your box.

9

TADA!
Pop your present inside, close the box and give it to an unsuspecting friend. Cue surprise, amazement and delight!

SWEET AS CANDY!

LET ME DO IT!

PIN-UP THAT DIAPER!

DIY EMOJIS

Design your own emojis for those times when the one you want just ain't there!

SWING TIME!

©MGA

GENIE POSTER

YOU WISH!

©MGA

HEADS UP!

Baby Cat and Fancy totally rock their awesome headwear! Can you design something new for them to wear? How about a flower crown, a hat or even animal ears!

MEOW!

MORE ISSUES THAN VOGUE

DRAW SOMETHING REALLY SILLY!

©MGA

HAPPY L.O.L.IDAYS!

What kind of vacay would suit your style? Take our fun quiz to find out!

1 WHEN YOU'RE TAKING A BREAK YOU LIKE TO:

a) Chill out completely.

b) Shop til you drop.

c) Keep busy.

2 WHAT DO YOU PACK IN YOUR SUITCASE?

a) Sunscreen, sunglasses and flip flops

b) A whole load of different outfits.

c) Your headphones.

3 WHAT'S YOUR IDEAL VACAY READING?

a) Your favourite mag.

b) The new book everyone's talking about.

c) You'd rather listen to some beats.

4 WHEN YOU HIT THE BEACH THE FIRST THING YOU DO IS:

a) Bag a lounger and settle down for the day.

b) See if there are any shops nearby.

c) Put on your beach playlist.

YOUR PERFECT VACAY MEAL IS:

a) A huge ice cream sundae.

b) A buffet with lots of different choices.

c) Whatever the locals are eating.

6

SIGHTSEEING TRIPS ARE:

a) A waste of time – you'd rather be by the pool.

b) OK as long as there's a gift shop.

c) Cool if you can listen to music on the way.

Mostly As

GOLDEN GODDESS

Vacays for you are all about relaxing. Just like Splash Queen, you adore chilling out by the pool or daydreaming on the beach. And the more the sun shines the happier you are!

Mostly Bs

FASHIONISTA

You love shopping, shopping and more shopping! The bright lights of the city would be your dream destination – there are just so many shops to choose from! And It Baby would love to be your vacay buddy!

Mostly Cs

M.C. VACAY

Just like Beats you like a soundtrack to your vacay. Whether you're chillin' at the beach, on a sightseeing tour or checking out the local cuisine, you're happy as long as you've got your headphones!

TRAVEL TIPS

There's so much to see on this crazy planet we call home! Make the most of your next trip away with these handy tips.

PLAN AHEAD

Do your homework like Teacher's Pet and research your destination before you go. You don't want to miss anything amazing just because you didn't know it was there! #travelswot

BEAT THE BOREDOM

They say the journey is as important as the destination but lots of travelling can get a little yawnsome! Pranksta would play jokes on her friends to liven things up but you could pack some travel games instead!

BECOME A BLOGGER

Write a travel blog so your BAEs know what an awesome time you're having on your trip. Neon Q.T. would love to read it! #makethemwelljel

TRY SOMETHING NEW

Travel is all about new experiences, especially if you're in another country with a different language, culture and cuisine. Be inspired by Sugar and Spice and try to do something that's the opposite to what you'd do at home!

ROCK THE MOMENT

Carry your phone or camera with you to take pictures but don't spend the whole time hiding behind the lens – try to be in the moment like Rocker would! #YOLO

FIT FOR A QUEEN

Glitter Queen is off on her travels. Design a new vacay outfit for her to squeeze into her suitcase.

I GLITTERALLY CAN'T!

TOP TIPS

Party planning is sooo much fun, especially when it's a surprise for a fabulous friend! These next few pages will help you plan the perfect bash for your BAE.

I DON'T DO GLAM, I AM GLAM

ZIP IT

Don't spill the beans! Surprise parties take a little more organising as you need to keep it a secret but all the effort is worth it just to see the look on your friend's face. Important things to remember are:

⭐ Make a fake date with your friend for the day and time of the party so you know that she will be free.

⭐ Tell all the other guests that it's a surprise so nobody gives the game away.

⭐ Have an outfit ready for her (especially if it's a themed party - she won't wanna be only one not in fancy dress!).

DREAM UP A THEME

Think outside the box! Themes are a great way to bring your party to life. Choose a fun idea that you know your friend will love. And don't forget to tell your guests who know about the party to come in themed fancy dress! Why not try one of these L.O.L. ideas:

I GOT GAME!

 An Opposites bash where everything is black and white.

 An Athletic Club sports day party with games and races.

 A red carpet celeb event fit for the Glam Club.

 A Retro party with your friend's favourite decade as the theme.

A Storybook celebration where every dresses as their favourite book character.

ALL ABOUT HER

Keep it real! Make sure your friend has THE best time at her party by making it personal to her and including lots of her favourite things. You could have:

 A table laid out with all of her favourite foods.

 A pop-up photo booth complete with props that tie in with your theme where she can take fun selfies with her friends.

 Personalised presents to give to her, such as sweets in a hand-decorated paper bag with her name on.

©MGA

PAGE 33

DAZZLING DÉCORS

The Glitterati have some super-cool decoration ideas to add a bit of sparkle to your surprise party.

YOU WILL NEED

HELIUM QUALITY BALLOONS

SCISSORS

CARDBOARD TUBES

SPARKLY CRAFT PIPE CLEANERS

CONFETTI

SPARKLING PARTY POPPERS

How to Make

1 Let's get started! Tie a knot in the end of a deflated balloon.

2 Time to snip! Cut a tiny bit off the top of the balloon.

3 Now streeeetch the balloon over the cardboard tube.

4 Almost done! Cut the pipe cleaners into small pieces (1cm to 2cm long) and pour into the open end of the cardboard tube.

5 Here's the fun bit! Pull back the knotted end of the balloon as far as it will go, let go and watch the sparkly pieces pop out.

TOP TIP! DECORATE THE OUTSIDE OF THE CARDBOARD TUBE FOR ADDED WOW FACTOR.

TOP TIP! REFILL YOUR PARTY POPPER TO USE AGAIN AND AGAIN.

TOP TIP! TRY OTHER FILLERS SUCH AS GLITTER (THIS WILL BE MESSY!), CONFETTI OR SMALL SPARKLY POM POMS.

CONFETTI BALLOONS

How to Make

1 Ok, let's go! Insert the funnel into the neck of a balloon.

2 Slowly does it! Carefully pour in about two tablespoons of confetti.

3 Pump it! Use a balloon pump to blow up the balloon then tie a knot in the end.

YOU WILL NEED

CLEAR BALLOONS
A FUNNEL
SMALL CONFETTI PIECES
A BALLOON PUMP

WARNING!

DON'T BLOW UP THE BALLOONS BY MOUTH AS YOU MAY INHALE THE CONFETTI.

GLITTER GARLANDS

How to Make

1 Time to begin! Draw around your jar to make lots of circles on glitter paper.

2 Concentrate now! Carefully cut your circles out.

3 Snip, snip! Cut the drinking straws into 1cm pieces.

4 Almost there! Tie a knot at the end of a long piece of string.

5 Alternatively thread glitter circles and straw pieces onto the string until your garland is the length you want.

6 Getting excited? Tie a knot at the end of the string and your glitter garland is ready to hang.

YOU WILL NEED

A JAM JAR OR SOMETHING ELSE CIRCULAR
GLITTER PAPER
SCISSORS
DRINKING STRAWS
STRING

©MGA

PARTY BAG GOODIES

MISS BABY

The fun doesn't have to stop when the party ends! Send your friends home with a party bag full of goodies. Here's an idea for a fabulous filler…

© MGA

YOU WILL NEED

CLEAR MELT AND POUR SOAP BLOCK (AVAILABLE FROM CRAFT SHOPS)

A MICROWAVABLE JUG

RECTANGLE SOAP MOULD

SMALL DECORATIONS

DIFFERENT COLOURED FELT

SCISSORS

CELLOPHANE

WARNING!

ADULT GUIDANCE IS NEED FOR THIS ACTIVITY.

How to Make

1 Snip snip! Cut a rectangular piece of felt the same size as your soap mould then cut other felt pieces to make a background.

2 Looking good! Arrange your felt pieces and decorations on a flat surface until you're happy with the design.

3 Chop chop! Cut the soap block into small pieces and put them in the jug.

4 Feeling hot! Heat in a microwave for 30 seconds or until the soap is melted but not boiling. Stir well.

5 Pour a thin layer (no more than 1cm) of melted soap into the mould. Leave to harden at room temperature for 30 minutes.

6. Almost finished! Once the soap has hardened lay the felt pieces and decorations on top of the base layer.

7. Re-melt the soap in the jug and fill the rest of the mould. Use a spoon to gently remove any bubbles.

8. Tada! Leave your soap to cool at room temperature until it's completely hardened (at least two hours) then push it out of the mould and package in cellophane.

DECORATION IDEAS

SMALL PLASTIC FIGURES

BUTTONS

BEADS

CHARMS

FOAM PIECES

BOWS

L.O.L. IT!

Fit for the Glitterati
add glitter to the soap mix and use sparkly sequins to decorate.

Opposites attract
use black and white felt, buttons and beads for a striking look.

Glam it up
try using animal print felt with diamante jewels.

© MGA

©MGA

FUN AND GAMES

The Theater Club have some mind-blowing magic tricks and a super fun unwrapping game to make sure your party entertainment's on fleek.

TOP TIP!

PRACTISE A TRICK BEFORE YOU SHOW ANYONE TO MAKE SURE YOU'VE GO IT DOWN.

COLOUR CHANGING DRINK

Amaze your guests with this colourful illusion.

1 Be discreet! In secret put a teaspoon of food colouring in the bottom of a non-transparent cup. Hide the food colouring under a whole load of ice cubes.

2 Ready to wow! Hold a bottle of water or clear lemonade aloft and pour it into the cup – when the liquid mixes with the food colouring it will 'magically' change colour. Tada!

FLOATING CUP

This simple cup trick will leave them asking how.

1 Bare all! Show your audience an empty styrofoam cup. Let them hold it and look inside it so they know it's a perfectly normal cup.

2 Set the scene! Take the cup in both hands and explain that you will try to make it float in the air.

3 Shake your thang! Move your hands up and down while shaking the cup as if you're trying to get it to float. Keep talking, explaining what you're doing.

4 Keep up the patter! Whilst moving the cup, discreetly push your right thumb through it so that the cup is attached to your hand – make sure you're talking at this point so that your audience doesn't hear the hole being made!

5 Catch that cup! Spread the fingers on your right hand and the whole of your left hand and keep moving your hands up and down as if the cup is floating away and you're catching it.

©MGA

TOP TIP!
REMEMBER THAT YOUR PERFORMANCE IS JUST AS IMPORTANT AS THE TRICK ITSELF – ADD LOTS OF DRAMA, ABRACADABRAS AND RAZZLE DAZZLE!

TURN WATER INTO ICE

Blow your guests' minds by turning water into ice in front of their very own eyes.

1 Time to chill! In secret put a bottle of water in the freezer. Take it out just before it reaches the point of freezing (after about two hours).

2 Cool as ice! Load up a bowl with a pile of ice cubes.

3 Your big moment! Hold your water bottle up high and pour the water over the ice cubes. Your audience will be wowed as the water turns to ice when it touches the ice cubes.

READ THEIR MIND

Your guests won't think it's possible but (with a little secret trickery!) it totally is.

1 Who you gonna choose? Pick a member of the audience and give them a pack of different coloured wax crayons.

2 Let the magic begin! Turn away from them and put your hands behind your back. Ask the person to pick a crayon and place it in your hands.

3 Time for some trickery! Turn to face them again but keep your hands behind your back. Distract them by talking about the trick you're about to perform while secretly scraping the crayon with your right thumb to get some wax stuck under your nail.

4 Razzle dazzle 'em! Keep the crayon behind your back in your left hand and wave your right hand in front of the person's face to 'transfer' their thoughts into your head. Sneak a peek at the colour underneath your right thumbnail.

5 Abracadabra! Amaze the audience by revealing your answer.

HIDDEN HEART CAKE

Every party needs a cake and it wouldn't be an L.O.L. cake without a hidden surprise! Your guests are guaranteed to love this sweet treat!

YOU WILL NEED

425G BOX OF RED VELVET CAKE MIX

425G BOX OF WHITE CAKE MIX

EGGS, OIL AND WATER AS PER INSTRUCTIONS ON CAKE MIX BOXES

HEART SHAPED COOKIE CUTTER

LARGE LOAF TIN

BAKING PAPER

TUBE OF ICING

SUGAR SPRINKLES

WARNING!

ADULT GUIDANCE IS NEED FOR THIS ACTIVITY.

How to make

1 Let's get started! Preheat the oven to 180°C/350°F/Gas mark 4 and line your loaf tin with baking paper.

2 Unbox it! Make the red velvet cake mix following the instructions on the box, pour into the cake tin and cook.

3 In the meantime, make up the white cake mix following the instructions on the box and put to one side.

4 Time to chill! Once the red velvet cake is ready take it out of the oven and leave it to cool. Then slice it into pieces about 2.5cm/1" thick and cut a heart shape from each slice. Freeze the heart shapes for 30 minutes.

5 Clean, dry and line the loaf tin again then pour about 1.5cm/½" of white cake mixture into the bottom.

6 Line up the love! Carefully place the hearts in a row along the length of the tin – they should be upright with the widest section at the bottom and close enough to touch.

7 Pour the rest of the white cake mix on top of the hearts making sure that the mixture doesn't come more than two thirds of the way up the sides of the tin.

8 Excited yet? Cook the cake according to the instructions on the box. Leave it in the tin until it's completely cooled then carefully remove.

9 Use a sharp knife to level off the top of the cake then turn it upside down – make sure you keep the cake this way round when you decorate it so that your hidden hearts are the right way up!

10 Now for the fun part! Cover the cake with icing and decorate with sprinkles. Now you're ready to surprise your friends with a cake they will love!

©MGA

SAY WHAT?!

The big sisters have sent their lil sisters secret messages. Can you work out what they say?

ANSWERS ON PAGE 48.

MY STYLE NEVER EXPIRES

1

SRAIGHT A'S 4 EVA

2

3

4

©MGA

5

....

HOW'S IT HANGING?

6

....

YOUR TURN!

Draw your own secret messages here.
Can your BFF work out what they say?

©MGA

TODAY IS:

WEDNESDAY

AND I'M FEELING:

CURRENT MOOD.
EMOJIS

1

Cut out the mood board template opposite and glue onto thick card.

2

Superglue two small wooden craft pegs onto your mood board where shown.

3

Carefully cut out the weekdays and emojis below and glue onto thin card.

Make this awesome emoji mood board to tell the world what kinda day you're having!

YOU WILL NEED

SCISSORS   GLUE   THICK CARD
THIN CARD   SUPERGLUE
SMALL WOODEN CRAFT PEGS

MONDAY

TUESDAY

WEDNESDAY

THURSDAY

FRIDAY

4

Prop your mood board up or stick it on your wall. Change the day of the week and emoji each day to show how you are feeling

SATURDAY

SUNDAY

©MGA

TODAY IS:

GLUE PEG HERE

AND I'M FEELING:

GLUE PEG HERE

THREE WISHES

Genie has granted one of the Glitterati three wishes. Use the clues below to work out who.

CRYSTAL QUEEN

QUEEN BEE

COSMIC QUEEN

GLITTER QUEEN

CLUE 1
SHE HAS GLITTERY HAIR.

CLUE 2
SHE'S WEARING BOOTS.

CLUE 3
SHE HAS BROWN EYES.

Wanna know what she's wished for? Hold this page up to a mirror and all will be revealed!

To always have friends who've got my back.

To be the best I can be.

To never stop believing in myself.

ANSWER
....

ANSWERS ON PAGE 48.

©MGA

SHHH, IT'S A SECRET...

Well it was but now it's time to spill the beans! Answer the questions below if you dare! #honestyisthebestpolicy

What is your most embarrassing moment?

Have you ever borrowed anything without asking?

What's the silliest thing you've ever done?

Have you ever broken anything and not admitted it?

What's the funniest thing you've ever done?

Have you ever made a mistake and covered it up?

©MGA

ALL THE ANSWERS

9 SONG SURPRISE

```
            G
            L
            A
            M
W O R K I T  I T U P
      C     M
      A     E
D A N C E I T O U T
      D     O
      Y     P
   S        A
   H O W W E R O L L
   A        T
   K        Y
W I S H
   I
   T
```

HIDDEN SURPRISE ANSWER

SHORTY

12 SCREEN SMASH
Luxe is calling

QUEEN BEE'S FAVOURITE WORD — **HONEY**

13 CHILLIN'

```
F S N O W M A N E
R S Y Z O C B K Y
E L B R R R A R L
E E C I R L R H L
Z D I T F S S C I
I G O W L O D I H
N F O N P H E R C
G N E F R O S T Y
S L L A B W O N S
```

SNOW ANGEL'S SURPRISE

BRRR IT'S COLD IN HERE

14 IT'S SHOWTIME!
In a world that's never dull, Genie, Pranksta and Coconut Q.T. decide to make things even more outrageous by switching places for a day! Cue a rollercoaster ride full of fun and oodles of surprises!

16 SAY THAT AGAIN!
What's the buzz Honey? Queen Bee
I rocked B4 I could walk! Rocker
Purr-fection! Kitty Queen
Straight A's 4 EVA! Teacher's Pet
Queen of the rink. Ice Sk8er
Chillin' with my homies! Brrr B.B.

17 SCRAMBLED SURPRISE!
1. Diva
2. Surfer Babe
3. Centre Stage
4. Honey Bun
5. Kicks
6. Cherry

42 SAY WHAT?!
1. Tea time
2. Cool as ice
3. Couch potato
4. Drama queen
5. Bombshell
6. Party animal

46 THREE WISHES
1. To be the best I can be.
2. To never stop believing in myself.
3. To always have friends who've got my back.
Answer: **Queen Bee**